This book belongs to

_____

The Cowgirl Way

Hats Off to America's Women of the West

by Holly George-Warren

Clarion Books
An Imprint of HarperCollins Publishers
Boston New York

clarionbooks.com

The text of this book is set in Hightower.
Photo credits are found on page 107.
Book design by Ellen Nygaard

The Library of Congress has cataloged the hardcover edition as follows:
George-Warren, Holly.
The cowgirl way: hats off to America's women of the West / by Holly George-Warren.
p. cm.
1. Cowgirls—West (U.S.)—Juvenile literature. 2. West (U.S.)—Social life and customs—Juvenile
literature. I. Title.
F596.G46 2010
920.70978—dc22

ISBN: 978-0-618-73738-3 hardcover
ISBN: 978-0-544-45595-5 paperback

Manufactured in China
22 SCP 10 9 8 7

For Robert and Jack,
who appreciate the cowgirl spirit;
for Ann Griffin, who first got me on a horse;
and in memory of Amy Hoban and
Teresa and Tyler Beard

✷ ✷ ✷

Contents

One of America's early cowgirls.

Introduction

"Always saddle your own horse!" That was the motto of Connie Douglas Reeves, a Texan who stayed in the saddle until her death at age 101 in 2003. An avowed cowgirl, Connie was part of a tradition that reaches back to the 1800s. Brave, independent, headstrong: women of the West demonstrated that they could tackle the same arduous tasks accomplished by their male counterpart, the cowboy. One hundred and twenty-five years ago, that meant riding the range, rounding up cattle, and capturing and taming, or "breaking," wild horses. Beginning in the early 1900s, some cowgirls also performed in rodeos, appeared in movies, and sang on the radio. Over the past century, cowgirls have owned ranches and raised cattle, horses, and sheep. Today, while some cowgirls still live on ranches and some perform in rodeos, others simply enjoy horseback riding as a hobby.

In the most literal sense of the word, a cowgirl is a woman, or girl, who works outdoors with livestock. In the nineteenth century, before the word "cowgirl" was coined, girls and women who learned to hold their own working with cattle and horses were sometimes called "cow-boy girls" as they helped settle the western frontier. It wasn't until around 1900 that "cowgirl" was commonly used to describe women who had become celebrated entertainers in Wild West shows and early rodeos.

More important than what cowgirls do with livestock, though, is a certain spirit that most cowgirls have: spunk, adventurousness, and courage. Some women who grew up on ranches, such as the former Supreme Court justice Sandra Day O'Connor, pursue other professions once they become adults. But they never stop being cowgirls at heart. Justice O'Connor made that clear in the book she wrote about her life, *Lazy B: Growing Up on a Cattle Ranch in the American Southwest*. In her native Texas, she had learned to ride and shoot by age eight. Her tenacity and spirit surely helped her become the first woman ever to be appointed to the highest court in the land.

✳ ✳ ✳

Connie Douglas Reeves teaching horseback riding at Camp Waldemar, in Texas, in the 1940s.

"I wish every American girl today could take a wagon trip [west]. Our young folks need the self-reliance we learned there. Nobody told us how. We set ourselves a job, then we did it. We used common sense. We helped one another. We didn't whine."

~Martha Jane Chappell, who traveled on a wagon train from Arkansas to California in 1869

Chapter One
Women of the Old West

Before anyone ever heard the word "cowgirl," there were women who ventured west. Most traveled with their families in covered wagons, beginning in the 1840s. They moved from crowded eastern cities to settle in western states such as Kansas, Nebraska, Colorado, Wyoming, Montana, New Mexico, Arizona, and Utah. Some wagon trains eventually went even farther, to California, Oregon, Idaho, and Washington.

After the Civil War, more and more people sought new lives in the West. For nearly thirty years, from the 1840s to the late 1860s, the largest migration in the history of our country took place. The Homestead Act of 1860 mandated that 160 acres could be claimed in the west by men as well as women as long as they were twenty-one and unmarried. Though men by far outnumbered women in the early years, by 1870, there were 172,000 women over the age of twenty out west, compared with 385,000 men.

While back east most women lived within society's traditional rules, pioneer women had to adapt to survive the harsh circumstances of their journey and new surroundings. Many began to take on chores formerly done only by men. Wives, widows, mothers, and daughters on farms and ranches were helping to settle the western plains. Some of these women homesteaders learned to master the skills of riding horses, roping cattle and other animals, and shooting a gun when necessary. Pioneer Nannie Alderson, who settled in Montana, believed that "the new country offered greater personal liberty than the old."

An unidentified woman scout of the late 1800s.

One new freedom for women that grew out of the pioneering way of life involved a change in wardrobe. In those days, women rarely wore pants, and when riding horses, they sat sidesaddle. Their skirts kept them from riding like men, and in any case it was not considered "ladylike" to do so. One early pioneer woman advised against observing customary attire and riding style while traveling to the West: "Sidesaddles should be discarded—women should wear hunting frocks, loose pantaloons, men's hats and shoes, and ride the same as men," she wrote. The work of settling the new frontier was leading many women to abandon (at least some of the time) the constricting, traditional mode of dress.

Ranch woman and photojournalist Evelyn Cameron wrote about her transition to buckaroo life in Montana and Wyoming in the 1880s. "For some twenty years past, there have been cowgirls on Western ranches who are the feminine counterparts of cowboys—riding in similar saddles, on similar horses, for the purpose of similar duties, which they do, in fact, efficiently perform. The abolition of the sidesaddle was naturally the first step towards the creation of the cowgirl . . . I [was] determined to ride astride. With [a] divided skirt, I found it a simple operation to mount into a cow saddle. So great at first was the prejudice against any divided garment in Montana that a warning was given to me to abstain from riding on the streets of Miles City lest I might be arrested!"

Young horsewoman Helen Bonham in Cheyenne, Wyoming, 1919.

"My impression of Montana was good, though different from anything I had ever seen. Edith and I spent most of the summer riding through the hills and over the prairie. How I enjoyed the little prairie dogs, who barked their welcome; the meadow larks who greeted us with their song, 'I'm here and can't get away'; the white-faced cattle that ran whenever they saw us."

~Homesteader and rancher Carolyn Janssen Bird

In the early 1900s, the cowgirl became a popular image on postcards and calendars.

"I generally can drive a few cattle alright. They do look lovely on the sunny slopes, all looking so happy and strong and handsome. . . . If you could only feel the rocking motion of a good lope through the grass and hear the creak of the saddle, and see the horses' fresh look after a long ride at this pace."

~Homesteader Mary E. Inderwick, 1884

In 1840, pioneer Sally Skull was one of the first women in Texas to own her own ranch, the Circle S, which she stocked with wild horses and cattle she brought across the border from Mexico. Her nickname was Mustang Jane, and her horse's name was Redbuck. Wearing men's clothing, she drove freight wagons from Texas to Mexico during the Civil War. A marker in her memory states that "she was a sure shot with the rifle she carried on her saddle or the two pistols strapped to her waist."

Another fearless cowgirl, Sarah "Sadie" Jane Creech Orchard, operated the Mountain Pride Stagecoach Line in 1886 and drove the treacherous journey from Kingston, New Mexico, to the Santa Fe Railroad terminal in Nutt, New Mexico. Known as the Belle of the Black Range, she later wrote: "The roughness and isolation of the Kingston-Hillsboro route was surely trying and a real test of my courage. I stayed alert, held tight to the reins, and rested my boot heel on the brake, ready to stop if the need arose. My old shotgun, nestled at my side, gave me an added feel of safety. I always thought the drive through the beautifully wild Black Range Country exciting and challenging. I never felt terribly in danger, although sometimes I could sense there were Indians and bandits lurking around."

A few women pioneers pretended to be men so they could live like cowboys. In 1867, Jo Monaghan traveled west by herself from Buffalo, New York. To reach her destination safely, she donned a pair of pants, a vest, and a hat, and passed herself off as a man. After settling down in Idaho, she found she liked doing ranch work. In part enjoying male privileges such as voting, and in part fearing the consequences of revealing her true identity, she kept her disguise. Jo worked hard and began buying enough land and livestock to start her own small ranch. Only upon Jo's death in 1904 was it discovered that she had pretended to be a man.

Gradually, more women went from working on ranches to owning them. One such enterprising Texan, Lizzie Johnson Williams, operated an enormous ranch in the late 1800s. In 1871, at age thirty-one, she first registered her cattle brand and began accumulating livestock. After marrying Hezekiah Williams, she realized she was sharper at the cattle business than her careless husband, and insisted that he sign an agreement giving her sole ownership of the property—a role reversal practically unheard of in those days. To further protect her interests, Lizzie joined her crew of cowboys to drive cattle up the Chisholm Trail. After a long, hard journey, she negotiated the sale of her livestock at their destination in Abilene, Kansas. This was another first for an American woman of the West, and Lizzie became known as the Queen of the Trail Drivers.

The farther west ranchers moved, however, the tougher it could be. Independent women often faced suspicion and harsh judgment on the part of their neighbors. Such was the fate of Ellen Watson, of Sweetwater Valley, Wyoming. Called Cattle Kate, she was accused of rustling (stealing) livestock in 1889. Local cattle barons greedy for her land killed her before she could even defend herself in court. The *Cheyenne Daily Leader* described the doomed woman: "Of robust physique, she was a daredevil in the saddle, handy with a six-shooter and adept with the lariat and branding iron . . . She rode straddle [rather than sidesaddle], always had a vicious bronco for a mount, and seemed never to tire of dashing across the range." A century later, historians found that Cattle Kate had been falsely accused of the crime and was innocent.

Kitty Wilkins, who became known as the Horse Queen of Idaho, fared better than Cattle Kate. Born in Oregon in 1857, she moved with her family to Idaho, where they began ranching. Kitty was an excellent rider, and her family bought her horses when she was still a girl. By the time

An unknown cowgirl from around 1900.

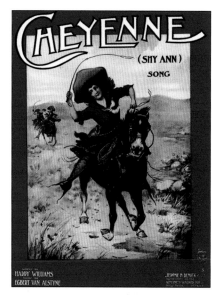

An early song, "Cheyenne," available on sheet music, popularized cowgirls.

she was twenty-eight, she had a herd of eight hundred. She made a fortune raising and selling horses. One cowboy later wrote of her tough reputation, "If a man weren't a good rider when he went to work for Kit Wilkins, he was a good rider when he left or he wasn't riding at all—*unless in a hearse.*"

Kitty's success is all the more amazing when you consider that for most of the nineteenth century, no woman in America could vote, run for public office, or own property. This began to change in the West, however, before anywhere else in the country. In 1869, Wyoming passed legislation that gave women the right to vote and hold civic office. The territorial assembly passed an act declaring that "every woman of the age of twenty-one years, residing in this territory, may at every election to be holden under the laws thereof, cast her vote, and her rights to the elective franchise and to hold office shall be the same under the laws of the territory, as those of electors."

The leader in the fight for women's rights in Wyoming was Esther Hobart Morris. Esther helped draft the women's suffrage bill there with William Bright. When the legislation was signed into law on December 10, 1869, newspaper headlines declared, FIRST WOMEN IN THE WORLD TO WIN EQUAL SUFFRAGE! The women of Great Britain sent a congratulatory telegram: "To the women of Wyoming on the triumph you have won for all women by the emancipation of the women of your state from political serfdom."

"**A**s soon as we children had mastered the art of sitting on a horse with some assurance, our value to the [cattle] business became out of proportion to our age. The art of horse-sitting is acquired rapidly if one keeps at it from daylight til dark, day after day, so we quickly learned to ride by the simple process of *riding*."

~ Rancher Agnes Morley Cleaveland

An unidentified cowgirl dressed in her western duds for a portrait photographer.

Also, in December 1869, Wyoming passed three other bills to protect and upgrade the status of women: they could now own property in their own name, they could earn money and keep it for the first time in history, and they could retain guardianship of their young children if their husband died. Esther Morris became the first woman to hold office in Wyoming Territory: in 1870, she was appointed justice of the peace in South Pass City. When she died on April 2, 1902, her son published her eulogy: "Her quest for truth in the world is ended, her mission in life has been fulfilled. The work she did for the elevation of womankind will be told in the years to come, when the purpose will be better understood."

Other western states and territories, including Utah, Colorado, Idaho, Washington, and California, began to follow Wyoming's example. Some of these states wanted to increase their population by encouraging women settlers to come west. It wasn't until 1920—fifty-one years after Wyoming spearheaded women's suffrage—that the Nineteenth Amendment was added to the U.S. Constitution, granting the right to vote to women across America.

Many women of the West recorded what pioneer life was like by keeping diaries and journals that were passed down from one generation to the next. Florence Bingham wrote that in 1871 her family homesteaded near the railhead cow town of Abilene, Kansas: "My pony was a swift traveler and I enjoyed many a fine ride over the vast prairie north of us where the antelope and other wild animals roamed. Because of the long-horned Texas cattle, it was not safe for anyone to walk."

Young Jennie Marcy lived on a farm near Baldwin City, Kansas, and wrote of discovering some ornery strays that crossed her family's homestead in 1878: "I, one of my father's 'boys' in this new country, [had] my very own pony, given to me for the express purpose of watching the fences, that no stray stock could 'break through and steal' our meager crops. [One day] I quickly mounted my pony and hurried my course through the deep, narrow ravine and climbed the hillside, where I completely surprised these Texas [longhorns] from the rear. I made my approach on the repulsive intruders like a Kansas cyclone with a shrill war whoop . . . I really succeeded in scaring the whole bunch of animals. . . . Three times I rounded them up and returned the unruly bunch to the place by which they entered."

Like Jennie, many girls who grew up on small farms learned to ride horseback so they could keep livestock from trampling their crops, locate their stray cattle, mend broken fences, and inspect watering holes. They also helped treat wounded steers, tended new calves, and milked dairy cows. Many came to love the way of life: "We would come up over the top of a hill into the glory of a beautiful sunset with its gorgeous colors, then down into the little valley already purpling with mysterious twilight," wrote Montana rancher Elinore Pruitt Stewart in 1909, looking back on her childhood. "So on, until, just at dark, we rode into our corral and a mighty tired, sleepy little girl was powerfully glad to get home."

A few skilled horsewomen decided to leave their families behind and became notorious figures whose fame still lives today.

"I am sitting beside my campfire tonight. My horse, Satan, is picketed nearby. You should see him—the light from the campfire playing about his sleek neck and satiny shoulders of muscle, white feet, and diamond of white between his eyes. He looks an object of all beauty. I am so proud of him."

~Journal entry of Calamity Jane, 1877

Chapter Two
Outlaws and Rebels

Though not exactly cowgirls, the two most infamous women of the West were expert equestriennes. Belle Starr and Calamity Jane both became "stars" of flamboyant early magazines called dime novels, which celebrated their notoriety. These colorful storybooks were popular throughout the country, and often featured real people as their heroes and heroines but exaggerated their exploits.

Myra Belle Shirley was born in 1848, the daughter of a Missouri businessman. As a girl, she attended private school and excelled in Latin, Greek, math, and spelling. Belle, as her parents called her, became a superb horsewoman. While in her teens, she made friends with some outlaws and ditched her traditional life. Legend has it that Jesse James was her pal and introduced her to his fellow gang member Cole Younger. She and Cole fell in love and had a daughter named Pearl. After Cole was killed during a bank holdup, she took up with another outlaw, Jim Reed, and together they had a son, Edward.

Some say that Belle traded her long dresses for men's clothing and participated in robberies. Others believe she simply hid her outlaw friends at her ranch after their crime sprees. Following the death of Jim Reed, Belle organized her own outlaw gang in Indian Territory, which later became the state of Oklahoma. She carried a Colt .45 revolver she called "my baby," and wore it in a holster around her waist. She took up with a Cherokee bandit named Sam Starr and became known as Belle Starr. The two were arrested

A young Calamity Jane around the time she served as an army scout.

"Were it not for the occasional musical notes of 'Calamity Jane,' our streets would be as orderly as any eastern city."

~Newspaper in Casper, Wyoming, 1889

in 1883 for horse theft and spent time in jail. A few years after her release, in 1889, Belle was shot in the back and killed by an unknown assailant. That same year, her embellished "biography" was published. Its cover showed her donning a cowboy hat and brandishing a six-shooter, and dubbed her "the Bandit Queen, or the Female Jesse James." Other stories referred to her as "the Petticoat Terror of the Plains."

Eight years younger than Belle, Calamity Jane was born Martha Jane Canary in 1856, near Princeton, Missouri. Her family joined a wagon train bound for Montana in 1864. After she became famous as Calamity Jane, she penned her life story (which she exaggerated) and recalled their journey West: "The greater part of my time was spent in hunting with the men and hunters of the party; in fact, I was at all times with the men when there was excitement and adventures to be had." By the time she was eight years old, she had become, according to Jane, "a fearless rider." By the time she was a teenager, her parents had died and she had to fend for herself. In 1870, she gave up petticoats and dresses for buckskin trousers and boots

Dime novels popularized the exploits of Belle Starr.

Elizabeth Montgomery took on the movie role of Belle Starr in 1980.

when she began traveling with the U.S. cavalry as a sort of mascot and fledgling army scout. In her autobiography, *Life and Adventures of Calamity Jane,* originally published in 1896, she wrote: "When I joined Custer I donned the uniform of a soldier. It was a bit awkward at first, but I soon got to be perfectly at home in men's clothes."

Around this time, according to her own account, she acquired her famous nickname by rescuing a Captain Egan during an Indian ambush: after she pulled the wounded soldier from his saddle and onto her horse and galloped back to the fort, he thanked her for saving him from such a calamity—and dubbed her Calamity Jane. Some, including Egan's wife, disputed this story. Others say Calamity Jane got the name because she was a troublemaker who caused disasters during her misadventures. Her nickname first made it into print in 1875, in the *Chicago Tribune.* That reporter gave yet another explanation for the moniker, stating that she had accompanied a military campaign to the Powder River but had wandered off, causing a scout to remark, "It would be a great calamity if she should be captured or killed by the Indians."

However she came by her famous name, there were two sides to Calamity Jane. One reporter wrote, "Whether a person was rich or poor, white or black, or what their circumstances were...her purse was always open to help a hungry fellow, and she was one of the first to proffer her help in cases of sickness, accidents or any distress." Though known for such acts of

Doris Day played Calamity Jane in the movies in 1953.

kindness toward hard-up or sick cowboys, she also drank too much whiskey. Once, while under the influence of alcohol, she rode a bull through the streets of Rapid City. She was arrested a few times for public drunkenness. But this less reputable side of her character only seemed to contribute to her legendary status, thanks in part to the dime novels' colorful coverage of her escapades. In one account, in a popular series called *Deadwood Dick*, author Edward Wheeler evoked the image of Calamity Jane: "[She] dressed in a carefully tanned costume of buckskin, the vest being fringed with the fur of the mink; wearing a jaunty Spanish sombrero; boots on the dainty feet of patent leather, with

Calamity Jane a few years before her death.

"Calamity Jane! The Fearless Indian Fighter and Rover of the Western Plains," in Deadwood!

"There is probably not a newspaper or magazine published in the United States [that has not printed stories] about Calamity Jane and her thrilling experiences and exploits of the western borders."

~*Black Hills Daily,* 1901

A young Pearl Hart.

tops reaching to the knees; a face slightly sunburned, yet showing the traces of beauty."

Calamity Jane was friendly with the famous army scout, hunter, and impresario William F. "Buffalo Bill" Cody. He later remembered her as a good hunter "perfectly at home in that wild country." During her adventures in Cheyenne, Wyoming, and Deadwood, South Dakota, she also nurtured a friendship with Wild Bill Hickok. When he was shot in the back during a poker game, she was heartbroken.

Sadly, Jane's hard-living ways caused her health to decline prematurely, and in 1903, at age forty-seven, she died. Calamity Jane was buried in Deadwood next to the grave of Wild Bill Hickok.

Belle and Jane may be the best-known nineteenth-century women of the West who lived outside the law, but they weren't the only ones. Pearl Hart, like Belle Starr, had to serve time in prison for robbery. The petite twenty-eight-year-old dressed in men's clothing, wore a cowboy hat, and carried a rifle to hold up a stagecoach. Newspapers called her "the Last of the Lady Road Agents." Claiming she needed the money to help her sick mother, she won the sympathy of the public.

Pearl's life had begun under normal circumstances. Born in Canada in 1871, she attended boarding school as a girl. At age sixteen, she eloped. Her husband was not much of a provider, and her life seemed on a downward turn. While the pair attended the World Columbian Exposition in Chicago in 1893, Pearl met some cowboys who impressed her with stories of the West. She left her husband and traveled to Arizona, where she found work as a cook in the numerous mining camps. Before long, Pearl headed down the outlaw trail. With a man named Joe Boot, she robbed a stagecoach. The law caught up with them and Pearl stood trial for robbery. A reporter for the *Arizona Star* wrote: "She is a wild-cat of a woman and had she not been relieved of her gun, a bloody foray might have resulted." Pearl was acquitted by a jury but had to stand trial again after the judge demanded she be tried for stealing the gun that belonged to the stagecoach driver. This time, in 1899, she was convicted, and was sentenced to do time at the frightening Yuma Territorial Prison as its first female inmate. Upon her release in 1904, Pearl changed her name, and eventually she married a politician in Arizona.

Pearl Hart after she became known as an outlaw.

The beautiful, cultured Etta Place became notorious for befriending the infamous Hole in the Wall Gang, or Wild Bunch, who robbed trains and banks across the West. She was particularly close to the gang's storied leaders, Butch Cassidy and the Sundance Kid. Though Etta was rumored to be a schoolteacher, her true identity and background have never been confirmed. Possibly hailing from Texas, she was an excellent rider and good with a rifle. Etta accompanied her boyfriend the Sundance Kid while he eluded the Pinkerton detectives who pursued him relentlessly. In 1901, Etta sailed with Butch and the Sundance Kid to South America, where she joined in their robberies. Together they managed to avoid capture for years. Etta vanished in about 1907, and to this day, no one knows what became of her.

Other women friends of the gang were Elizabeth Bassett and her daughters, Josie and Ann. The Bassett family owned a secluded ranch near an area called Brown's Park, at the border of Colorado and Utah. There, Butch Cassidy and other Wild Bunch members sought refuge from the law. Both Bassett daughters attended private school in Salt Lake City but preferred ranching life to gentility. Ann knew how to use a lariat, and at age thirteen, she roped a grizzly bear cub. When the mother bear charged her, she hoisted herself up an aspen tree, escaping harm.

Ann Bassett's early acquaintance with outlaws may have influenced the choices she later made. As an adult, she became known as the Queen of the Rustlers, a name she earned by stealing livestock from wealthy cattle barons. She told her side of the story in her 1952 memoir, *Queen Ann of Brown's Park*. In the chapter called "Scalawag," she fondly recalled the first calf she ever rustled: "In the spring of 1883, I found a dogie that was left by the mother when the [cattle] drive passed our ranch. . . . The wild little brute was full of fight, but I managed to get it to the house, over a distance of a mile, which took most of the day and a lot of relays. After I fed the calf milk, I went to Mother and told her about my find. When she saw the starved, tiny creature that had been branded and ear-marked at that tender age, she immediately made it clear to me that I could feed and care for the calf, but as soon as it could eat grass and grew strong enough to rustle its living without milk I must turn it on the range, for I knew very well that it belonged to Mr. Fisher." Ann went on to say she loved the calf, named it Dixie Burr, and fought to keep it, even changing its brand to conceal its true ownership.

Ann's sister, Josie, had a crush on Butch Cassidy, who spent time reading books in the Bassett ranch library. She later wrote of him, "I thought he was the most dashing and handsome man I had ever seen. I was such a young thing . . . and looked upon Butch as my knight in shining armor. He was more interested in his horse than he was me." Josie's

Etta Place became famous through her friendship with the outlaws Butch Cassidy and the Sundance Kid.

greatest passion, though, was the land, and after their mother's death, she and Ann maintained ranches until they died of old age.

The Bassetts, who loved to ride, shoot, and rope, like many women pioneers, never demonstrated their talents to the public. But a new breed of independent-minded women were learning the ropes of "show business." By becoming popular entertainers, these professionals helped to spread the fame of the cowgirl around the world.

"Let any normally healthy woman who is ordinarily strong screw up her courage and tackle a bucking bronco, and she will find the most fascinating pastime in the field of feminine athletic endeavor."

~May Lillie, star of Pawnee Bill's Wild West

Chapter Three
Wild West Show Girls

Calamity Jane's friend Buffalo Bill Cody helped to bring to life some of the people depicted in dime novels, including daring women on horseback wielding firearms. As the founder of the hugely popular Buffalo Bill's Wild West Show in the 1880s, he staged dramatizations of western history and featured performers who could ride, shoot, and rope like nobody's business. One of the biggest stars of his show was Annie Oakley, who paved the way for many other female western entertainers.

Annie Oakley was born Phoebe Ann Moses in rural Darke County, Ohio, in 1860. Her father died when she was eight years old, and she helped put food on the table with the rifle he had left her. She honed her marksmanship by bagging quail, pigeons, turkeys, geese, rabbits, and other small game, and sold what her family did not need to the local butcher shop and restaurants. Her precision with a gun gained her local fame. At age fifteen, she competed in shooting contests against men twice her age. She later said, "When [the men] saw me coming along they laughed at the notion of my shooting against them. . . . It kind of galled me to see those hulking chaps so tickled in what was no doubt to them my impertinence in daring to shoot against them—and I reckon I was tickled too when I walked away with the prize."

By the time she was twenty, the petite Phoebe could beat anybody at competition shooting, including roustabout marksman Frank Butler. After she bested him at a prestigious shooting contest in Cincinnati, she

GRAY PHOTO
BOSTON.

ANNIE OAKLEY

Annie Oakley wearing the
many medals she won for
marksmanship.

Annie Oakley in action.

decided to team up with Frank and put on shooting exhibitions around the country. Before leaving Cincinnati, she took the stage name Annie Oakley. Within a year, she and Frank had married, and he became her manager and assistant while she starred in various traveling shows. In 1885, Annie auditioned for Bill Cody, who was thrilled by her prowess with a gun and signed her to his show, Buffalo Bill's Wild West and Congress of Rough Riders of the World. She was nicknamed Little Sure Shot by another headliner, Sitting Bull, the legendary chief who had defeated General Custer. Soon, Annie added trick riding to her repertoire. Her act included such feats as shooting through a dime held in her husband's hand and firing at an apple on her poodle's head. By using a mirror, she could also hit a target behind her back.

When Buffalo Bill took the Wild West Show to England for the first time in 1887, Annie was billed as "the Peerless Lady Wing-Shot." In London

The largest share of applause was bestowed on Annie Oakley, a young girl whose proficiency with shotgun and rifle seems almost miraculous.

~*London* (Ontario, Canada) *Free Press,* September 2, 1885

A poster for the Buffalo Bill's and Pawnee Bill's Wild West Show, featuring cowgirls.

she met Queen Victoria, who told her, "You are a very clever little girl." The troupe also traveled to Rome and Paris. One spectator later described Annie's effect on her audiences: "She was a consummate actress, with a personality that made itself felt as soon as she entered the arena. Even before her name was on the lips of every man, woman, and child in America and Europe, the sight of this frail girl among the rough plainsmen seldom failed to inspire enthusiastic plaudits." Annie worked with Buffalo Bill for sixteen years, earning as much as a thousand dollars a week.

Annie Oakley was so popular with audiences that Buffalo Bill added other women to his troupe, whom he advertised as

A gathering of Wild West Show performers.

LIFE AND ADVENTURES OF BUFFALO BILL
ACTUAL SCENES IN MOVING PICTURES BY CODY HIMSELF

A 1912 advertisment for an early movie featuring Buffalo Bill's Wild West Show.

"What we want to do is give our women even more liberty than they have. Let them do any kind of work that they see fit, and if they do it as well as men, give them the pay."

~Buffalo Bill Cody, 1899

"a bevy of Beautiful Rancheras, genuine and famous frontier girls." Among them was equestrienne Emma Lake Hickok, Wild Bill Hickok's stepdaughter, who performed a square dance on horseback. Another star attraction, Georgia Duffy, was billed as "the Rough Rider from Wyoming."

Numerous touring Wild West shows emerged in the late 1800s, including one operated by Gordon "Pawnee Bill" Lillie. Pawnee Bill's Wild West featured "beauteous, dashing, daring, and laughing Western girls who ride better than any other women in the world," according to his show posters. One of his stars was his wife, May Lillie, of Philadelphia, who had graduated from Smith College. Hailed as the "Champion Girl Horseback Shot of the West," she rode traditional sidesaddle style, but that didn't prevent her from astounding audiences with her riding, shooting, and roping stunts.

Some of Buffalo Bill's Wild West Show cowgirls.

Martha Allen and the Parry sisters, members of the 101 Ranch Wild West Show.

Posters claimed she was "the only lady horseback shot." She performed in her husband's show for twenty-five years. Bertha Blancett, who had grown up working on her father's Colorado ranch, also joined Pawnee Bill's show. Later, Bertha became a pioneering rodeo star.

By the turn of the century, there were an estimated eighty touring companies of Wild West shows. Florence Hughes Randolph, from Oklahoma, started her own outfit, Princess Mohawk's Wild West Hippodrome. The Kemp Sisters' Wild West Show, which toured in the mid-1890s, also was operated by women. Texas Rose was the rare female announcer of the Texas Kid Wild West Show in the 1920s.

One of the most influential and longest-running acts was the Miller Brothers 101 Ranch Wild West Show, which evolved from a large cattle ranch in Bliss, Oklahoma. The 1912 program for the show boasted about the troupe's "Wild West Girls Whose Throne is the Saddle . . . an element new

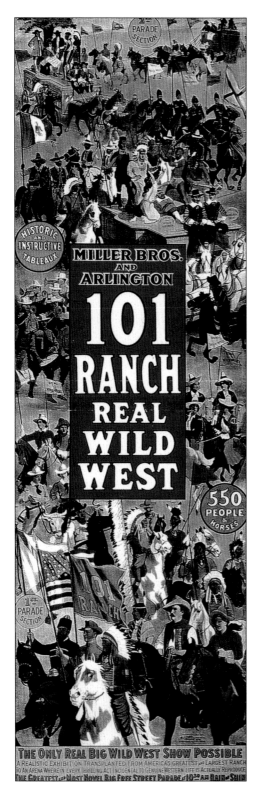

An early promotional poster for
the 101 Ranch Wild West Show.

to this community." It described the show's typical female star as a "lively, athletic young woman with a superfluity of nerve and animal spirits, with a realization that in affairs where skill is the chief qualification she has an equal chance with her brothers." By 1913 the 101 Ranch employed fifty women, including Wenona, "the Champion Indian Girl Rifle Shot," who was actually a non-Native woman named Lillian F. Smith. Sometimes billed as "the California Girl Champion Rifle Shot of the World," Lillian had started her career at age fifteen, with Buffalo Bill. She competed against Annie Oakley on horseback as part of the show. Wenona found stardom at the 101 Ranch, where she shot target after target while astride a galloping horse.

Another star of the 101 Ranch lived a double life. Jennie Woodend was a Manhattan socialite who adopted the name Jane Howard in order to appear as a trick rider with the show. The daughter of a wealthy doctor, she had learned

Some of the cowgirls and one of the cowboys featured in the 1915 version of the 101 Ranch Wild West Show.

to ride as a child. But as the wife of a man who disapproved of her cowgirl aspirations, she took a stage name to appear with the 101 Ranch. Her true identity was discovered in 1911, after she was thrown from her horse, Chester, while performing in a Brooklyn arena. When she was treated by a doctor for a sprained ankle incurred in the fall, the news leaked out. New York City newspapers ran such headlines as RANCH GIRL, INJURED, REALLY MRS. WOODEND and EQUESTRIAN'S FALL REVEALS IDENTITY. In 1920 she gave up city life for good and moved to the 101's home ranch in Oklahoma. She no longer performed but worked as a cowgirl, riding horses and mending fences. Years later, a member of the Miller family remembered her as the top cowgirl of the troupe: "She was spectacular," he said. "She rode in the shows and she rode the fences. You should have seen her ride."

Lulu Parr, of Cheyenne, Wyoming, was one of the 101's most extravagantly dressed performers, known for her fringed calfskin riding skirts, gorgeous beaded vests, and matching long gloves. Female Wild West performers, not to be outdone by Buffalo Bill's fancy costumes, wore eye-catching hats, boots, and colorful outfits. Women's wearing pants was still frowned upon, but thanks to cowgirls, that would soon change. For now, split riding skirts had to suffice.

The Wild West Show performer Lulu Parr in one of her beautiful outfits.

Another well-known star of the 101 Ranch was the first of the western gals to be called "cowgirl" in print. In 1899 the famous humorist and entertainer Will Rogers and the future U.S. president Teddy Roosevelt met thirteen-year-old Lucille Mulhall at the Oklahoma ranch of her father, Zack. Lucille was a superb rider and roper, and could outperform her father's cowhands in lassoing and roping calves. She had started riding at age two, and by the time she was eleven, she had mastered the art of roping, with her captives eventually including steers, jackrabbits, and wolves. Treated to demonstrations of Lucille's prowess on horseback, observers such as Teddy Roosevelt and Will Rogers went back east raving about her accomplishments. So when Papa Mulhall decided to wrangle Lucille and her sisters, Bossy, Georgia, and Mildred, and her brother, Charley, into joining a family Wild West troupe, they had a ready-made audience.

During a 1904 tour that included a stint at the St. Louis World's Fair, Lucille broke steer-wrestling records by roping, dropping, and tying three steers in just over two minutes. The Mulhall show, the Congress of Rough Riders and Ropers, hit New York the following year, winning Lucille more

"You could get $25 a week working for a Wild West show. I used to let out the rope over my head and pop it til it roared. Then I'd take a matchbox off Dakota Bob's head. I enjoyed it. It went so fast, and it was so fun, I never had time to stop and think. We were on the go all the time."

~Alice Renner, star of Warner's Western Review

Lucille Mulhall at the 101 Ranch.

legions of fans, along with such titles as "the Lassoer in Lingerie" and "Champion Lady Steer Roper of the World." In 1905, at age nineteen, she became a star attraction at the 101 Ranch. That year, in Kansas, she beat thirty-eight cowboys in a three-day steer-roping contest. She could rope as many as eight galloping horses with one lasso. Lucille's horse, Governor, performed such tricks as playing dead, ringing a bell, removing her hat with his teeth, walking on his knees, and crossing his legs.

Lucille soon had many friends performing in the 101 Ranch, including Ruth Roach, Mabel Strickland, Tillie Baldwin, and Mildred Douglas. These courageous and bold women were poised to apply their skills to another form of entertainment that has lasted to this day—rodeo.

View by Jedrica

The first "cowgirl,"
Lucille Mulhall.

"**If** I can just get my fanny out of the saddle and my feet planted, there's not a steer that can last against me."

~Champion steer wrestler Fox Hastings

Chapter Four
Rodeo Stars

Though Calamity Jane was criticized for her reckless bull-riding high jinks, when undertaken by cowboys such escapades became a major attraction of rodeos. These tests of cowboy skills started growing in popularity around the same time Buffalo Bill organized his first Wild West Show. Originally called Stampedes or Frontier Days, organized events developed out of cowboys' casual competitions—using their horses, cattle, and lassos—at the end of the roundup. The ranch hands would see who could ride the most ornery horse, who could rope a calf the quickest, and who could ride and tie up a bull. Fancy trick riding was part of the repertoire, too, so early rodeos were quite similar to Wild West shows. Instead of performing for pay, however, cowpokes earned prize money by competing against one another. And from the beginning, young ranchwomen such as Lucille Mulhall showed they were every bit as capable as the cowboys at such matches.

Several locations claim to be the site of the first rodeo. In 1888, Prescott, Arizona, staged the first of its Frontier Days, which has occurred every year since. In 1893, in Lander, Wyoming, the first commercial rodeo was promoted in which prize money was given to winners of the competitions. Though these initially excluded women from competing, a rodeo in Fort Smith, Arkansas, did permit a young equestrienne named Annie Shaffer to ride a bucking horse in its 1896 event. The following year, in 1897, opening day of the Cheyenne competition was almost rained out. But Bertha

Trick riding contestants, circa 1930.

Blancett kept the audiences in their seats by being the only person at the Cheyenne Frontier Days willing to ride a bronc in the muddy arena. According to cowgirl chronicler Joyce Gibson Roach, "The cowboys decided that if a woman could ride in such conditions, they had better do it too." So it was on with the show! The rodeo's organizer later recalled his impressions of the horse Bertha rode: "One of the worst buckers I have ever seen, but Bertha stayed on him all the time. Part of the time he was up in the air on

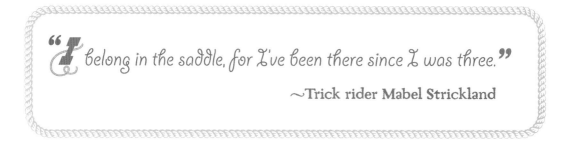

"I belong in the saddle, for I've been there since I was three."

~Trick rider Mabel Strickland

Prairie Rose Henderson and a favorite horse, around 1920.

his hind feet; once he fell backward and the girl deftly slid on one side to mount him again as soon as he got up. She rode him to the finish."

Most rodeos still tried to keep women out, however. Prairie Rose Henderson, the daughter of a Wyoming rancher, put up a fuss when the Cheyenne organizers barred her from competing in 1901. She demanded to see the rodeo rules, which did not prohibit women's entry in contests. In addition to insisting on riding that year, she "created such a sensation

Bertha Blancett riding the bucking horse Eagle at the 1914 Pendleton Roundup.

that many of the rodeos soon included as a feature event a cowgirls' riding contest," says one rodeo historian. Three years later, Cheyenne officially permitted women to compete. Bertha Blancett returned that year and wowed the crowds with the stunts she performed on her horse Tombstone.

Women who had already gained fame through Wild West shows, circuses, and informal local competitions continued to lobby hard for their inclusion in *all* rodeos. Finally, by 1906, "ladies' bronc riding" was added to most rodeo programs. Lucille Mulhall began competing and won lucrative prizes, including a thousand dollars for best steer tying at one Texas rodeo. A spectator reminisced: "Lucille looked about eighteen and wore a divided skirt. First woman I'd ever seen that wasn't on a sidesaddle. She was a fine steer tier. She could rope those steers, drag 'em down, and tie 'em just like a man." Lucille weighed only about ninety pounds at the time.

Lucille Mulhall.

Thanks to the efforts of Bertha Blancett, Lucille Mulhall, and Prairie Rose Henderson, women were invited to participate in the 1911 Pendleton Roundup and the 1912 Calgary Stampede the first year they opened. Many female contestants came into prominence performing there, and more U.S. rodeos began accepting women. Mabel Strickland won top prize in several categories. Born in 1897, she began her career relay-racing horses, then became a champion trick rider beginning in 1913. The next skill she mastered was roping, and by 1922, she had won the trophy for "Best All-Around Cowgirl" at the Cheyenne Frontier Days.

Fanny Sperry Steele, "Lady Bucking Horse Champ of the World" in 1912 and 1913, perhaps best described the cowgirl spirit in a 1976 reminiscence: "How can I explain to dainty, delicate women what it is like to climb down into a rodeo chute onto the back of a wild horse? How can I tell them it is a challenge that lies deep in the bones. . . . Perhaps it is odd that a woman should be born with an all-consuming love of horseflesh. . . . It seems to me as normal as breathing air or drinking water, that the biggest thing on my horizon has been the four-legged critter with mane and tail."

Bonnie Gray was a talented pianist and had earned a college degree in music, but she chose to compete in rodeos and became a frequent champ. One of her stunts included jumping with her horse King Tut over an

Fanny Sperry Steele was one of the female pioneers appearing at rodeos—here and opposite, in 1913, at the Winnipeg Stampede.

automobile filled with people. Rodeo work was dangerous and hard, but adventurous women liked the challenge. "I rode forty-two bucking horses in one week," Fanny Sperry Steele recalled about her stint at a rodeo in Milwaukee. "We put on eleven shows a day. I rode in six bucking events every day for a solid week, but I loved every minute of it."

The 1933 Madison Square Garden Rodeo presented numerous women in the "bronk riding contest," in which the winner could earn $2,775 ($200 less than her male counterpart). That year's program stated, "There are probably about 50 young women who [compete] for glory and cash prizes at various rodeos. . . . Most of them are ranch bred, and have broken wild

"Sometimes it takes a lot of grit to do what you want to do."

~Rodeo star Fanny Sperry Steele

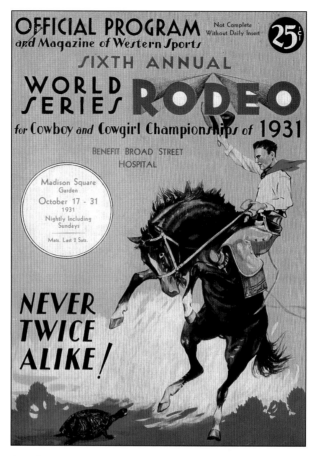

A rodeo program from Madison Square Garden, 1931.

horses in the corral or on the open range. The pick of these cowgirls are appearing at the Garden Rodeo. In the cowgirls' bronk riding, the same rules apply as in the cowboys' bronk riding. The bronks ridden by these daring young women are real 'outlaws.'"

Trick riding was just as difficult as riding a bucking horse. As the horse galloped along, a cowgirl would leap up to stand on its back, and would also hang off its side or even pass underneath its belly. In "chariot

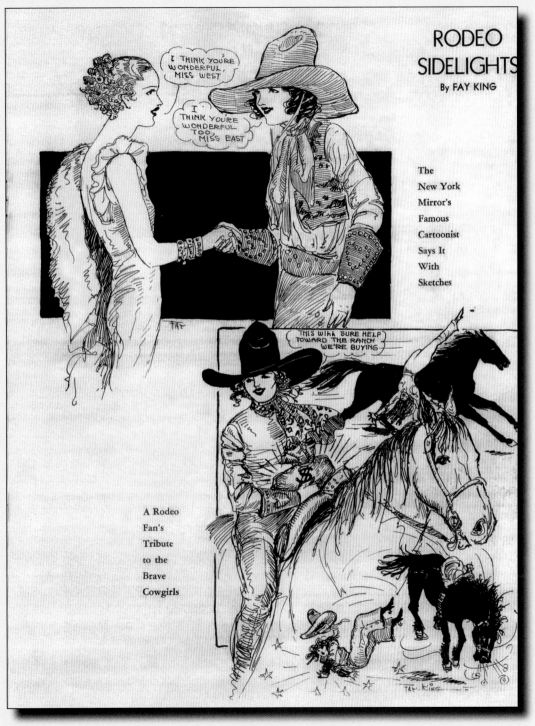

Cartoons depicting cowgirls featured in a 1931 rodeo program.

Tad Lucas with her prize saddles and trophies at home in Texas in the 1920s; sadly, many of these were destroyed in a fire in the 1930s.

racing," a woman would ride standing on two horses running side by side with one leg on each horse. In relay racing, three horses ran around the ring and the cowgirl jumped from one horse to the next.

Tad Lucas with baby Mitzi, 1928.

Tad Lucas, once described as "the world's greatest female rider," was among the group of women who gained fame for their spectacular trick riding. Born Barbara Barnes, the youngest of twenty-four children in Nebraska in 1902, she began her rodeo career in 1924 and went on to win dozens of trophies. In 1933, she was severely injured when she was stomped on by her horse's hooves while doing a trick. Her left arm was so badly broken that it had to stay in a cast for three years, and she never fully regained the use of her arm. It was at this time that her six-year-old daughter, Mitzi, who had started riding at age two, began performing with her.

"She shattered her arm doing a trick," Mitzi Lucas Riley relates. "The doctor told her that it would never be strong or well again, but she could do some things with just one arm. That's when she let me go into trick riding." Mother and daughter worked together for twenty years, and Mitzi never

"I always thought my mother had the cowgirl spirit, because nothing ever kept her down. You always say, 'I can do it better.' That's the cowgirl spirit."

~Mitzi Lucas Riley, speaking of her mother, Tad Lucas

Fox Hastings, a champion bulldogger and All-Around Cowgirl.

"This is the life I've been looking for, the continual challenge! I love it."

~Rodeo champ Vera McGinnis

broke a bone. "I took many a spill," she says, "and I'd have a sore shoulder or aches and pains that came along with it. But not enough to put me out of showing. I had a good teacher, and I knew how to fall—to a point. And my horses were trustworthy. I trained them myself."

Fox Hastings was the rare woman who excelled at "bulldogging," a dangerous feat in which the contestant wrestles a steer or bull to the ground, then ties his legs together. "When I see that ole steer come charging down the track, I almost shudder with fright," the redheaded Fox told a newspaper reporter in the 1920s. "But in a moment it is over, as I leap from my horse and make a catch for the steer's horns. Then there is the tussle to pull the steer's neck over. No wonder it is called 'steer wrestling' as well as 'bulldogging.' I've had lots of bones broken and I'm not foolish enough to think I won't break a few more. But there's a thrill in bulldoggin'; I like it!"

Cowgirls appearing at the Cheyenne (Wyoming) Frontier Days, 1929.

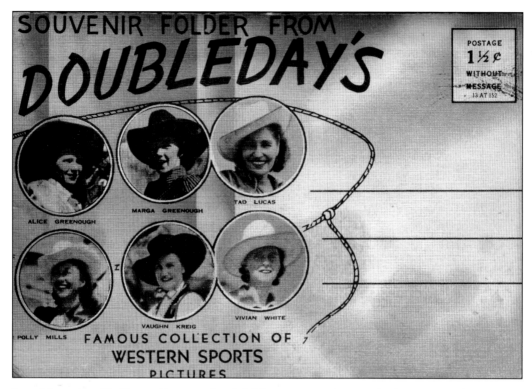

SOUVENIR FOLDER FROM

DOUBLEDAY'S

POSTAGE
1½¢
WITHOUT
MESSAGE
· 13 AT 152 ·

ALICE GREENOUGH

MARGA GREENOUGH

TAD LUCAS

POLLY MILLS

VAUGHN KREIG

VIVIAN WHITE

FAMOUS COLLECTION OF
WESTERN SPORTS
PICTURES

Cowgirls such as Tad Lucas (top row, far right) became very famous in the 1920s and '30s.

A San Franciscan who was educated in a convent, Fox learned to bull-dog by helping to "mug down" (wrestle to the ground) cattle for branding at a rodeo promoter's ranch, which she visited with her rodeo champ husband. The promoter "noticed her great strength and agility," according to a Houston, Texas, newspaper report, "and suggested she try it in the arena. She immediately became enthused over the idea, with the result that since coming to Houston she has downed three longhorns in practice and says she is ready to show the public that bulldogging is also a woman's game." The paper ran a photo of Fox flexing her biceps. Fox could throw a thousand-pound steer in twelve seconds and frequently beat the male contestants.

Over the course of four years, Fox broke her leg twice while springing from the back of her horse Buster to grasp the bull by the horns. Both times, after recovering, she returned to performing, and she was declared All-Around Cowgirl of the World at the Madison Square Garden Rodeo. She told a reporter, "I was the first woman with the nerve to try bulldogging. And I built the stunt to a point where it has great value as an attraction in Chicago, New York, and in Canadian arenas."

The daredevil women who braved bucking horses, galloping stallions, and ferocious steers became wildly popular with audiences. They

Margie Greenough Henson came from a family of prize-winning cowgirls and cowboys.

Montana-born cowgirl Alice Greenough specialized in risky trick riding.

risked their lives and seemed to love every minute of it. But after a tragic accident at the 1929 Pendleton Roundup, in which bronc rider Bonnie McCarroll was killed during the bucking horse competition, rodeos began gradually eliminating the "dangerous" categories for women contestants. Some rodeo historians have speculated that during the Depression, when funding was limited, women were pushed aside so that the men could earn the scarce prize money. Steve Friesen, director of the Buffalo Bill Museum and Grave, has theorized, "I am convinced that women were eventually excluded from the bronco riding competitions because they were better at it than the men. The men used the fatal accidents as an excuse to get rid of the competition."

Most rodeo promoters were male, and they began sponsoring "ranch girl" or "glamour girl" contests, in which women were judged more for their looks than for their courage and skill. Fearless competitors such as Tad Lucas who despised such equestrienne beauty pageants stopped competing and became judges of the male rodeo contestants. One of the top bronc-riding cowgirls, Montana's Alice Greenough, recalls, "Nineteen forty-one was the

"**I** have a great philosophy of life. Do all you can as fast as you can. If I had to do it over, I'd do the same thing, only a little more of it."

~Rodeo star Fern Sawyer

last year they had girls' bronc riding in New York. At one time New York had something like seventeen girl bronc riders entered [at the Madison Square Garden Rodeo]. After '41, a few shows had exhibition girls bronc riding, but that just about ended the competitive era."

By 1942, the brand-new barrel racing category had been devised for women contestants. It took enormous skill to race a horse around a maze of barrels without knocking any over, but it wasn't as exciting as riding a treacherous bucking horse or tackling a bull. Yet when so many male rodeo stars joined the service during World War II, women barrel racers took the spotlight in the arena. "That's when they started using more women in more events," recalls Mitzi Lucas Riley, who first performed at the Madison Square Garden Rodeo in 1943. "And girls' rodeos started about that time. The women held the rodeo together until the guys got back," she says.

After World War II, women's rodeo organizations formed to help save the tradition of women in rodeo. The Women's Professional Rodeo Association (WPRA) is the oldest organized group for women athletes in America. A few women-only rodeos still permit cowgirls to compete in the arena, including riding bucking horses and bulls, and roping and tying calves, and barrel racing continues to be the major category for cowgirls in today's pro rodeo. Arizona's Kim Williamson is one of the top All-Around ropers in the history of women's rodeo. "The mental aspect has to be there if you want to win," she advised in 2007. "Life is too short for negativity. This is a pretty tough world we live in—so you've got to reach for the positives."

In the twenty-first century, rodeo remains a popular and ever more lucrative sport. And many heroic and brave cowgirls helped to create this enduring and exciting western spectacle.

Bronc rider
Alice Greenough,
around 1932.

"I remember doubling for a star on the Beverly Hills bridle path one day and doing five falls off a cantering horse for ten bucks a fall. But I was glad to get the work. My only complaint was there wasn't enough of it."

~Trick rider Mabel Strickland

Chapter Five
Celluloid Cowgirls and Singing Sensations

Rodeos and Wild West shows were not the only entertainments to feature cowgirls in the early twentieth century. Thanks to the movies, radio broadcasting, and recordings, people from all over the country could see and hear cowgirls. This helped to spread the popularity of the West and encouraged girls living in cities and small towns to dress like cowgirls and, in some cases, actually become cowgirls.

In the earliest days of filmmaking, Annie Oakley starred in a predecessor to movies, the Edison Kinescope. Over the next few decades, Annie Oakley, Calamity Jane, and Belle Starr became the subjects of numerous movies and theater productions and were depicted by a variety of actors.

Some real cowgirls moved from trick riding in arenas to stunt work in the movies. Del Jones was one of the first trick riders to make this transition. Born Odille Osborne, she left home as a teenager to work in a Wild West show. At the Miller Brothers 101 Ranch, she met the dashing Buck Jones. In 1915, the two were married in a horseback ceremony. They became star attractions with the 101 Ranch and moved to Hollywood after World War I. Del started doing stunt work in Westerns, doubling for movie star Douglas Fairbanks in the 1919 film *The Knickerbocker Buckaroo*.

Odille Jones was one of the first cowgirls to be in both Wild West shows and the movies.

Another Wild West show star featured in movies was May Lillie. In *Queen of the Buffalo Ranch*, she played the owner of a ranch who eventually captured the outlaw, rescued her kidnapped niece, and gained a reward from the state of Oklahoma. An advertisement for the film stated: "May Lillie needs no introduction—her worldwide reputation gained through her remarkable feats at shooting targets from the back of a running horse and her wonderful mastery of the horse gained her notice and an acquaintance with the public that will never die."

Ruth Mix, the daughter of cowboy movie star Tom Mix, acted in a handful of Westerns. Ruth had earlier performed in rodeos and Wild West shows and was an accomplished equestrienne. Other rodeo performers who occasionally appeared in movies include Bertha Blancett, Vera McGinnis, Bonnie Gray, Florence Hughes Randolph, and Mabel Strickland. Mabel started as a stunt woman and then starred in twenty-four short episodic movies called serials, including *The Girl from Flamingo* and *Women's Ways*. She also appeared in *Rhythm on the Range* with singing star Bing Crosby in 1936.

> *"I had the rodeo fever, so I left Hollywood and went back to Texas."*
>
> ~Trick rider Florence Hughes Randolph

Mabel Strickland was known for roping steers, but she also starred in some Hollywood movies, doing trick riding and stunts.

The first actress to take on the cowgirl role in a series of silent movies was the feisty "Texas" Guinan, who knew how to ride and rope. Born Mary Louise Cecilia Guinan in Waco, Texas, in 1884, she started her career as a chorus girl in New York City music halls. To make a name for herself, she donned black lace chaps and trotted down a ramp on horseback through a Times Square theater, twirling her lasso. Sure enough, "after the show a movie man signed me up [for] a two-reel western," she later recalled. She starred in such films as *Get Away Kate* in 1917, *Two Gun Woman* in 1918, and *The Girl Sheriff* in 1921.

Barbara Stanwyck in the role of Sierra Nevada Jones in 1954.

In 1935, Annie Oakley provided a major role for Barbara Stanwyck, one of Hollywood's most renowned actresses. Born Ruby Stevens in 1907 in Brooklyn, New York, the actress-to-be was an orphan at age four and spent her childhood in foster homes. As a little girl, she earned coins by dancing in the streets to the sounds of a hurdy-gurdy (a hand-cranked music machine). Her entry into show business began in the chorus at the Ziegfeld Follies, followed by a musical revue organized by Texas Guinan. After acting in a Broadway play, Barbara moved to Hollywood in 1928. In 1935, she was cast in her first Western, *Annie Oakley*. Four years later in *Union Pacific*, she played the spunky daughter of a train engineer and did all her own stunts, a feat she would repeat throughout her career. Costar Joel McCrea enthused that she was "fearless and has more guts than most men." Barbara loved action roles, and in 1950, in *The Furies,* much to the director's dismay, she insisted on doing her own risky riding scenes rather than let a stunt double handle them. She once boasted, "I'm the best action actress in the world. I can do horse drags and jump off buildings, and I have the scars to prove it."

Dorothy Page was Hollywood's first singing cowgirl.

One of Barbara's favorite roles was Sierra Nevada Jones, a headstrong cowgirl who drives cattle from Texas to Montana with her father in *Cattle Queen of Montana* (1954). Playing opposite future U.S. president Ronald Reagan, Barbara earned the respect of her Blackfeet Indian colleagues by doing all her own stunts. After the shoot, they awarded her with membership in their Brave Dog Society, citing her "very hard work—rare for a white woman," and giving her the honorary title Princess Many Victories.

Barbara took on a total of ten Westerns in the 1940s and 1950s, including the roles of outlaw women in *The Maverick Queen* (1956) and *Forty Guns* (1957), originally titled *Woman with a Whip.* Her best-known role was California rancher Victoria Barkley on television's *The Big Valley,* which ran from 1965 to 1969. Barbara's strong-willed western woman influenced the next generation of actors, such as Jane Fonda, Anjelica Huston, and Jane Seymour, who would also play cowgirls in movies and on television.

Hollywood's first singing cowgirl was Dorothy Page, who began her career on the radio. She was cast in the role of ranch gal Shirley Martin, who captured outlaws in a string of late-1930s Westerns, including *Water Rustlers, Ride 'Em Cowgirl,* and *The Singing Cowgirl.* Early musical Westerns starring Gene Autry often featured cowgirls in key roles. In some of the movies, cowgirls worked on dude or guest ranches or cattle ranches. Roy Rogers and other cowboys made films that featured saddle gals played by June Storey, Peggy Stewart, Jane Frazee, Penny Edwards, Sheila Ryan, and others, some of whom were superb riders. Teenager Mary Lee, who started singing at age twelve with a swing band, became one of Gene Autry's favorite costars. She popularized cowgirl outfits and horseback riding among young girls, who flocked to see her in Autry films in the late 1930s and early 1940s.

The most famous of all the singing cowgirls in films was Dale Evans, who was crowned by fans "the Queen of the West." Ironically, the Texas-born singer-songwriter-actor grew up dreaming of being a Broadway chanteuse rather than a singing cowgirl. A few years after her birth in 1912, Lucille Wood Smith moved with her family from Uvalde, Texas, to rural Arkansas. She loved to make up songs and sing and dance as a young girl. Working as a singer in Louisville and Chicago, she changed her name to Dale Evans. In 1941, she went to Hollywood, and three years later she starred in *The Cowboy and the Senorita* (1944) with singing cowboy Roy Rogers.

Though she hit it off with her costar, Dale did not get along with her horse. She later recalled: "I had not ridden since I was seven years old. The fact was I couldn't ride worth beans. To make matters worse, they gave me a big horse with the disposition of a convict breaking out of prison—frisky to the point of being downright mean and with a mind of his own. How I stayed on my horse I'll never know. I bounced so hard in the saddle that

"Oh, thank heavens for Dale Evans."

~The Dixie Chicks

CLOCKWISE FROM TOP LEFT: Cindy Walker, a Texas songwriter playing a singing cowgirl (front, left), and Mary Lee (front, right) in a scene from *Ride, Tenderfoot, Ride,* 1940; Caren Marsh as a cowgirl in the 1940s; Mary Lee with Gene Autry in *The Singing Hill,* 1941; Penny Edwards starred opposite Roy Rogers in the '40s and on Western TV shows in the '50s; Sheila Ryan played a cowgirl in numerous movies and television programs.

THE SINGING HILL

Dale Evans became a good horsewoman thanks to her horse Buttermilk.

my temporary caps just flew out of my mouth." Fortunately, Roy encouraged his costar to get riding lessons, having said, "I never saw so much sky between a woman and a horse." Dale was given a more compatible horse named Pal, followed by her most famous horse, Buttermilk.

Roy and Dale married in 1947 after Roy proposed while the two were appearing at a rodeo. They made twenty-eight films together, and Dale's character was always smart, independent, and outspoken. She played such roles as journalist, scientist, novelist, entertainer,

Dale Evans paper dolls became popular in the 1950s. CENTER: Dale Evans and Buttermilk. RIGHT: Dale Evans played opposite Roy Rogers, her husband in real life.

"For me, the spirit of the cowgirl was contagious. The cowgirl's independent character suited me. I was, after all, a Texan."

~Dale Evans

Gail Davis played a cowgirl in movies with Roy Rogers and Gene Autry.

Gail Davis dressed as her TV character Annie Oakley.

and ranch owner. Her trademark cowboy hat, cowgirl outfits, and boots made the western style of dress popular among women all over the country. Though she was a great star, in the film credits she usually took fourth billing, after Roy, his "costar" Trigger, "the Smartest Horse in the Movies," and Roy's sidekick, Gabby Hayes. Nevertheless, Dale became the only woman to place in the Top 10 Most Popular Western Stars poll voted on by movie theater owners.

Among her many achievements, Dale wrote several important songs, including Roy Rogers's theme song, "Happy Trails." Gene Autry made a hit record of her composition "I Wish I Had Never Met Sunshine." Many children grew up singing her song "The Bible Tells Me So."

When Dale took a break from acting after the birth of her baby girl in 1950, Gail Davis took her place in a Roy Rogers movie. Gail went on to costar opposite Gene Autry. An Arkansas native who attended college in Texas, Gail often played a feisty cowgirl in Autry films such as *Whirlwind* (1951). She appeared

Gail Davis starred opposite Gene Autry in Western movies in the 1940s and '50s.

Gail Davis merchandise became popular among Annie Oakley fans in the 1950s.

in fourteen Autry movies, more than any of his other leading ladies. In 1953, Gail was cast as the lead in a new TV series, *Annie Oakley,* becoming the first woman to star in a Western on television. The first show opened with Annie doing a trick riding sequence (actually performed by her stunt double, the great equestrienne Donna Hall). The program's mostly fantasized depiction of Annie Oakley found her living with her kid brother, Tagg, near the dusty desert town of Diablo. Wearing cowgirl garb decorated with bull's-eye targets and accentuated with fringe, the pigtailed sure shot wrangled with unscrupulous tinhorns and deadly train robbers, proving that women *could* get the job done, though she usually had to prove it every week to her skeptical deputy sheriff pal, Lofty. The show aired for three years in syndication, from January 1954 to February 1957. During this time, Gail also performed in Gene Autry's touring company, astounding audiences with her own trick riding skills and target shooting. She even replicated the real Annie Oakley's stunt of shooting at a target with her back turned and using a mirror.

✳ ✳ ✳

Patsy Montana recorded the million-copy-selling record "I Want to Be a Cowboy's Sweetheart" in 1935.

A decade before Dale Evans became a famous singing cowgirl, women were crooning and yodeling the songs of the West. One of the first of these performers was Patsy Montana, whose composition "I Want to Be a Cowboy's Sweetheart" became a cowgirl anthem in the 1930s. Before the emergence of yodeling cowgirls, women who sang country music usually worked in family groups. It was frowned upon for female singers to travel on their own, without a father, husband, or uncle along for "protection." When Patsy Montana became successful as an independent performer, yodeling the songs of the West, she broke down barriers. She won the freedom to travel as a headliner around the country, appearing on radio programs and in the movies. It seemed "cowgirls" could get away with a more venturesome lifestyle than previous female singers. Soon, more and more women artists were following in Patsy's footsteps.

Born Ruby Rebecca Blevins in rural Arkansas in 1908, Patsy grew up as a tomboy surrounded by ten brothers and doting, hard-working parents. Her mother and father recognized her musical talent

A songbook featuring Patsy Montana's festive songcraft.

"Sweetheart of the Saddle"

BY PATSY MONTANA

~ ✱ ~

I'd like to see my cowboy pals
And live a life that's free.
I'd like to wear again my Stetson hat
And ride on the lone prairie.
There's something about the West that gets me
And beckons with a lure that's strong.
I'd like to sit and dream by a campfire's gleam
Singin' this western song.

I had never felt so free and independent in my life. I was working and earning a little money at something I loved, making music. To share this new life with two wonderful friends, as close as real sisters must be, was absolute heaven. The Montana Cowgirls did not care where we performed, as long as we were working and having a good time with our music. . . . All three of us, being single, went anywhere at a moment's notice. We wore matching suede skirts, blouses, boots, and western hats. We looked good and sounded good, with two violins and a guitar. Ruth, Lorraine, and I rode horses, and we rode motorcycles. We played in mountain snow, the blue waters of the Pacific, on the giant Redwood trees of the Yosemite National Forest. We worked together, ate together, played together and were as one. "

~Singing cowgirl Patsy Montana

early on and provided their daughter with violin lessons. She became quite a fiddler and entered talent contests in high school. After graduation, she traveled west to live with a brother and his wife in Los Angeles. There, she sang and played guitar while attending the University of the West (now UCLA). After winning a talent show on a local radio station, she garnered bookings as "Rubye Blevins, the Yodeling Cowgirl from San Antone." Popular western singer-songwriter Stuart Hamblen invited her to join his troupe, which included trick roper Montie Montana and the Montana Cow-

Louise Massey popularized western songs on radio in Chicago and New York in the 1930s.

girls, Lorraine McIntire and Ruth DeMondrum. Ruby changed her name to Patsy Montana and became part of the first-ever singing cowgirl trio to broadcast on a California radio station. The Montana Cowgirls also made a series of short films. In 1932, Lorraine and Ruth decided to give up show biz to get married, so Patsy returned east.

During the summer of 1933, Patsy and her brother traveled to Chicago, where the World's Fair was in progress. Patsy took along a huge watermelon from her folks' Arkansas farm to enter in a contest at the fair. Her primary goal, though, was to audition for a spot on the Chicago radio station WLS. Stars on the WLS *National Barn Dance* program included Gene Autry (before he became a movie star) and other groups who performed cowboy songs. Two of the most popular were Louise Massey and the Westerners, a family of former ranchers from New Mexico, and the Girls of the Golden West, composed of the Missouri-born Good sisters, Dolly and Millie. Also

Patsy Montana (in polka-dot blouse) and the Girls of the Golden West (Millie and Dolly) were among the cast of the WLS Barn Dance traveling troupe in the early 1930s.

at WLS, an expert string band, the Prairie Ramblers, wanted a female lead singer. Patsy Montana auditioned and got the gig. Her theme song with the group was "Montana Plains."

While on the road one day, Patsy had an idea for a new song. "I Want to Be a Cowboy's Sweetheart" emphasized her zesty yodel and her independent streak, with the lyrics "I want to learn to rope and to ride." Backed by the Prairie Ramblers, she recorded the song in August 1935. It steadily grew in popularity, eventually reaching one million in sales—the first time a female artist had accomplished such a feat. The song received even more exposure when it was featured in Gene Autry's 1939 hit movie *Colorado Sunset*.

For the rest of her life, Patsy performed as a singing cowgirl, influencing several generations of women to dress in western outfits and sing about the West. "By popularizing the cowgirl image, Patsy Montana gave female country performers their first new solo vocal style," write music historians Mary Bufwack and Robert K. Oermann.

In the far northeastern state of Maine, Janet McBride began yodeling as a child in the 1940s. "It was 1942 and I was eight years old," says Janet, "and I had dreams of being the best dern country yodeler in the land." She and her brother and sister started a singing group in rural Maine, called the Lister Trio. Janet began recording as a solo artist in the 1960s, and her specialty was yodeling. She particularly loved the songs of Patsy Montana, and the two became friends. Janet's first hit came in 1965 with her own "Yodeling Jan." Nearly twenty-five years later, then living in Texas, Janet coached seven-year-old LeAnn Rimes. "When her recording of 'Blue' hit the airwaves," says Janet, "the word got out that I helped her learn to yodel and I started getting calls from young people around the country who wanted me to teach them, too."

Devon Dawson supplied the vocals for Jessie the Yodeling Cowgirl on the *Toy Story 2* soundtrack.

Devon also performs and records with the Texas Trailhands.

With long red hair, a huge cowboy hat, fancy cowgirl shirts, fringed skirts, and decorated boots, Devon Dawson looks as if she could have been a Wild West star *and* a singing cowgirl of the movies. Based in Fort Worth, Texas, Devon performs all over the country with her group, the Texas Trailhands, which includes her husband, Chuckwagon Chuck. "My hubby is a fifth-generation Texan," says Devon, "descended from ranchers in the Red River country along the Chisholm Trail." Devon started playing guitar at age nine and began performing professionally at twelve, and likes to ride horses in her spare time. On the album *Woody's Roundup Featuring Riders in the Sky*, she sings western songs as Jessie the Yodeling Cowgirl. In 2001, the CD won a Grammy as Best Musical Album for Children. Dressed as Jessie, she performed around the country and introduced cowgirl songs to the fans of *Toy Story 2*. With the Texas Trailhands, she yodels western classics as well as new songs written by the band.

In 2007, Devon recorded *Keepin' Your Head Above the Water*, which pays tribute to the famous rodeo cowgirls of Texas. She and

Devon Dawson and yodeling cowgirl Janet McBride (back row, far right) teach kids how to yodel in Fort Worth, Texas.

Janet McBride teach kids how to yodel at the Cowtown Opry in Fort Worth. "It is my belief, and Janet's, that most anyone has a yodeler buried deep inside," says Devon. "We also ask our buckaroos to learn the history of their songs, for music is the expression of a people and their culture."

Every year in Texas and Oklahoma, there are yodeling contests in which new singing cowgirls are discovered. Seventy-five years after she first sang "I Want to Be a Cowboy's Sweetheart," Patsy Montana's legacy lives on in every cowgirl's yodel.

"**W**e all had lots of clothes. We always wore our best clothes, no matter what we were doing. If we had to ride a bull or a bucking horse or anything else, we wore our best clothes, we sure did."

~Champion trick rider Tad Lucas

Chapter Six
Cowgirl Image Makers

Everyone recognizes a cowgirl thanks to her distinctive wardrobe: a cowboy hat, cowboy boots, and often a flashy western shirt with piping and decorative embroidery. The cowgirls who performed in the early Wild West shows and rodeos were exciting to watch, and many wore huge hats and eye-catching flashy clothes. Beginning in the 1920s, cowgirls popularized trousers and short bobbed hair, as did their flapper sisters back east. Flamboyant dressers like Prairie Rose Henderson and Fox Hastings helped to create a colorful western style soon taken up by cowboys.

In a 1934 Madison Square Garden rodeo program, author Damon Runyon described cowgirl fashion: "[They] wore the costume made famous by Annie Oakley—buckskin blouse and skirt and leggings, all nicely fringed. They took up the idea of introducing color into the rodeo, and now they're togged out in silk blouses and tight-fitting satin trousers. . . . These girls can ride—there's no doubt about that. . . . The fact that they go in for color just proves that the cowgirls are human, like other dolls." Chances are Prairie Rose and Fox didn't appreciate being called dolls!

Many of the rodeo women designed and sewed their own costumes. Del Jones recalled, "One of the girls in the [101] was a seamstress, and she made a lot of our clothing. She made this coat and I just loved it. I had long red hair at the time and when I rode into the show arena I could

**Prairie Rose Henderson popularized bloomers and pants for
cowgirls with her festive garb.**

feel my hair blowing in the wind and that fringe with the beads tapping me gently on the back." Trick rider Mamie Francis found a tailor in Pennsylvania to stitch her designs, and after she recommended him to friends, he became a popular custom western-wear designer and assumed the name Rodeo Ben.

Florence Hughes Randolph was a well-dressed cowgirl from Oklahoma.

Mamie Francis was a trick rider who helped start the career of Rodeo Ben, a legendary designer of show clothes.

Another custom tailor got her ideas for western wear by riding the range herself. Marge Riley grew up on a ten-thousand-acre ranch in Wyoming and enjoyed riding. In the 1930s, she began fashioning fringed suede jackets, knee-length split skirts, and fancy western shirts for herself when she couldn't find what she wanted in local shops. When friends from neighboring ranches began commissioning outfits, her business took off. In 1936, she opened a shop in Los Angeles, which attracted such customers as Dale Evans, Roy Rogers, and Gene Autry. Her fashions were featured on the cover of *Life* magazine in April 1940.

The same issue of *Life* also ran a feature on the popularity of cowboy boots and the companies that produced them. One of these companies was founded in Nocona, Texas, by Enid Justin. Born in 1894 to bootmaker

One of Marge Riley's designs and fancy boots featured in *Life* magazine.

H. J. Justin, she grew up amid the craft of hand-making boots. Her father developed a mail-order system that extended the customer base beyond his shop in Nocona. Enid and her brothers went to work for their father's company, and at fourteen, Enid designed her first pair of boots, inspired by a pattern in a velvet brocade couch.

After her father's death, Enid's brothers moved the Justin Boot Company to Fort Worth, in July 1925. Enid wanted to keep her father's memory alive in Nocona, so she stayed there and, two months later, started the

In this April 22, 1940, issue, *Life* magazine featured cowgirl fashions, including designs by Marge Riley, a cowgirl herself.

"For rough ranch life, denim frontier pants, which are similar to but tighter than blue jeans, and cotton shirts are most used."

~ *Life* magazine, April 1940

Cowgirls' Bronk Riding Contest

For the Championship of the World
—Purse $2,775.00

The final winner of this event will be presented with a silver punch bowl by Ranch Romances Magazine

"I WANT to enter the bronk ridin' contest. I c'n ride any bronk that any man c'n ride, and I don't see how you're goin' to bar me out."

The speaker was a determined looking young ranch woman, and she was laying down the law to the committee arranging for one of the first Rodeos in Cheyenne, Wyo., back in the late '90's, when such contests were just getting started.

The committee didn't know about letting a girl ride a bronk. It never had been done, but, after all, there didn't seem to be any good reason why it couldn't be tried out. So, Wyoming being one of the first woman suffrage states and all that, Prairie Rose Henderson, such being her name, got her chance at bronk riding. She went out and rode whatever horse she drew, for Prairie Rose didn't ask any odds of the cowboys. She "rode slick"—that is, without hobbled stirrups, and she rode so well that she got in the prize money. After that she became a

regular contestant at Rodeos, and for several years Prairie Rose Henderson, in her Annie Oakley suit of fringed buckskin, was a familiar figure at these contests in the West.

Today Prairie Rose Henderson would have found lots of competition in the matter of bronk riding at Rodeos. Since her day, cowgirls' bronk riding has become a regular feature of the Rodeo program. Plenty of daring girls from far western ranches began to appear in Rodeo competitions. Pretty soon they had an event all to themselves—the Cowgirls' bronk riding contest—which proved to be one of the most popular contests on the bill.

The rules governing the cowgirls' bronk riding contest are practically the same under which the cowboys ride. The only exception that is made in favor of the cowgirls is that their stirrups are hobbled—that is, they are fastened down by a rope passed from one stirrup to the other, under the horse.

A group of cowgirl contestants—all experts in the saddle

This rodeo program article featured Prairie Rose Henderson and other Madison Square Garden cowgirl contestants.

Nocona Boot Company. In the beginning, ranchers and cowboys didn't want to buy boots from a woman, and Enid struggled to get enough business. Her sister, Myrl, traveled with her across Texas to sell boots, and they created a tall lace-up pair that became a hot item among oil field workers. Enid dreamed up other inventive designs: a favorite pattern was called

Madison Square Garden Rodeo Ranch Girl contestants and entertainer Gene Autry show off an array of western styles, 1950.

"the Neck," inspired when she sat at a funeral behind an elderly man with a heavily wrinkled neck. She sketched the design then and there, and a new boot style was born.

In the 1930s, Enid gained almost as much celebrity as the rodeo cowgirls of the 1920s. The 1936 Texas Centennial Exposition made cowboy boots more popular than ever, and Nocona Boots became a huge commercial success, making Enid wealthy.

During World War II, austerity measures enforced by the government required that boot manufacturers make only black and brown boots, with no fancy designs and colors or stitching on the boots' toes. Incensed, Enid contacted government officials to demand a hearing to allow her to put stitching on the toes: "I got the boot people together and we went up there to Washington and convinced them the stitching was functional, not just decoration," Enid told a reporter. The stitching helps to increase the boots' durability, Enid explained, so that cowpokes can stand on their toes in stirrups and put pressure on that part of the boot. "We got that [restriction] changed," she proudly said.

With the success of her company, Enid could have retired. Instead, even in her eighties, she refused to stop working and warned, "I'll not let the rockin' chair get me! I've got too much to do to be worryin' about myself." She lived to be ninety-six years old.

I developed a trait that has stood me in good stead all my life—just plain, mule-headed persistence.

~Boot maker Enid Justin

CLOCKWISE FROM TOP LEFT: Cowgirls backstage at the Madison Square Garden rodeo, circa 1950; Alice (left) and Margie Greenough getting ready to appear at the Garden arena, 1938; a woman's magazine cover featuring a cowgirl; a selection of Nocona boots, 1940; Katy K (for Kattelman) began designing western wear in the '80s and in the '90s opened a Nashville shop, Ranch Dressing, which also featured vintage western wear, modeled here by Brenda Colladay; the late Amy Hoban designed beautiful embroidered western clothing inspired by Dale Evans's outfits in the 1940s and '50s.

Hearst's International
COMBINED WITH
Cosmopolitan
OCTOBER · 25¢

Beginning a Series of Novelettes of New York Life
by **Faith Baldwin**

Katy K
PRESENTS
The Grand Opening Of
RANCH/DRESSING
FEATURING
Dos Cajones
Saturday, Nov. 12, 1994
7:00-9:00 pm

113 17TH AVENUE SOUTH
(OFF BROADWAY)
NASHVILLE, TN 37203
PLEASE RSVP 259-4163

**Wild West show star Lulu Parr favored lavish beaded
vests with matching hatband, armbands, and gauntlets.**

Today, there are still a handful of women boot makers—including
Lisa Sorrell, who crafts handmade custom boots in Guthrie, Oklahoma. A
few women continue to create western outfits reminiscent of those made
by Marge Riley. Such companies as Katy K's Ranch Dressing in Nashville,
Tennessee; Double D Ranchwear in Yoakum, Texas; and Amy Hoban's
Californiawear in Los Angeles, California, were all founded by women who
want to keep the cowgirl look alive.

"Cowgirl costumes are practical but ultra-feminine. The cowgirl costumes, braided and embroidered and worn with bright blouses, are all made of pastel flannels and tailored ∼ the girls hope ∼ to stand up under the toughest wear. That's quite a trick of tailoring, considering the way the clothes fit."

∼Bess Stephenson, reporter for the
Fort Worth Star-Telegram, c. 1932

"I've known a lot of cowgirls in my life. Rough, tough, fearless, and always with the biggest hearts I've ever known. Whether they are in the arena, the corrals, or out in the pasture, they know what to do. And because they are women, they have to do it three times better than any man there, to prove themselves and be accepted."

~Reba McEntire

Chapter Seven
Twenty-First-Century Cowgirls

Cowgirls are not as numerous as they once were, but women today still work on and own ranches. We see cowgirls in the movies and on TV, and we sometimes hear their music on the radio. There are a few Wild West shows that feature cowgirls. Women continue to participate in rodeos, and they raise and train horses. Cowgirl and scholar Teresa Jordan, who grew up on a Wyoming ranch, traveled all over America to interview more than one hundred cowgirls for her book *Cowgirls: Women of the American West*, first published in 1982.

"I don't know how many cowgirls live in the West," she wrote. "Every ranch community I visited boasted at least one. Many had several." About her own early years, Teresa wrote, "I rode before I could walk. By the time I was seven or eight, each summer my older brother and I rode every day, either alone or together, and looked after the cattle. I grew up surrounded by women and girls who worked on the range, right beside their husbands and brothers."

When she revised her book in 1992, Teresa discovered that "the increased visibility of women on ranches is one of the most pronounced changes of the past ten years." More women had attained positions of power in ranching and agricultural organizations, and more women ran or worked on ranches. Changes in our agricultural system and economy over the past few decades, however, have made it more difficult to operate small ranches

Scottie McTeer, a young cowgirl taking part in a Douglas, Wyoming rodeo.

today. Many girls who grow up on ranches have to find work elsewhere to make ends meet. Yet despite the hard work and long hours, and the economic challenges of ranching, many girls still choose to carry on their family tradition as best they can. The work includes haying, moving cattle, participating in roundups, branding calves, and training horses.

Perhaps because of the powerful and enduring image of the cowgirl, women continue to leave city lives behind to work on a ranch. One such

Photographer and cowgirl Jean Laughton lassoes a calf for branding.

adventurer is Clover Hughes, who in 2006 wrote an essay about her time on the JA Ranch in Texas: "Texan summers are mercilessly hot, but the monotony of the unstinting heat and dusty days spent on ceaseless fencing projects was broken by the drama and glamour of the rodeo season. Tutored by the cowboy foreman, Billy, and the ranch cowboys, Brooks, Lane, Randy and Jimmy Jack, I learnt how to ride bucking horses. Although completely wild, the two-year-old colts were roped, saddled, and ridden within a day. Sometimes violent and almost always dangerous, bronc-riding remains the true stamp of a cowboy's grit and determination in this macho world. I loved the intoxicating rush of adrenaline as I rode a wild pony for the first time, the thudding of blood in my ears and the taste of it in my mouth as I struggled to stay on. Usually, all too soon, the sand of the arena would rush up to meet my outstretched hands, and the cowboys would shout at me to get back on again." Clover gave up bronc riding after she turned twenty-seven and had a baby.

"**I** have a special feeling for this land. My mother and father came here to ranch in 1911 and it is where I was born, grew up, and lived all my life. . . . I know what it's like to ride all day and never encounter another person . . . to drive cattle home in the fall and have them strung out for two or three miles heading for winter pastures . . . to have a horse get loose and leave me fifteen miles from home. I am as much a part of this land as the coyotes and gophers."

~Rancher Marjorie Linthicum

Jean Laughton surveying her herd in South Dakota.

Iowa-born Jean Laughton had worked as a photographer in New York City before traveling west to find new subjects. She enjoyed taking portraits of women rough-stock riders who competed in rodeos. During a visit home, she was surprised to discover that in the 1940s and '50s, her great-grandmother had been friendly with several rodeo stars and had photographed them. In 2001, Jean's western portraits were featured in a group exhibition in New York that included the legendary rodeo photographer Louise Serpa. "Louise was the first woman granted the privilege to photograph action in the rodeo arena," Jean reports on her website. "It was an honor to have my work beside hers and to find out she had even photographed a relative of mine rodeoing back in the 1960s!"

The day came when Jean "wanted to be on the other side of the camera" herself, and in 2002, she moved to Interior, South Dakota, where she learned to ride and to work cattle. Eventually, she purchased a small herd and began working her cattle on a historic ranch dating to the 1880s that's been in the same family for generations. She loves "learning all aspects of cowboying," she says. "Getting into the ranching business changed my life completely—I am now 'in the photograph.' It is quite a feeling to ride across

Tavia Stevenson riding bareback at a rodeo in Wall, South Dakota.

the same White River and across the same pastures herding cattle as they did back in the day." Jean still takes photographs, including wonderful portraits of rodeo cowgirls and scenes from her own life working on a ranch.

Texan Lisa Leann Dalton didn't become a rodeo performer until age forty. She had spent nineteen years as a modern dancer when she decided to ride bucking broncs. "Ever since I was five, I have been horse crazy," she said in 2006. "So I told my family I was retiring from dancing and either taking up bronc riding or racing horses." Leann returned to her hometown of Fort Worth, got a job at a stable, and started practicing. During her first year competing, she began winning prizes. Leann competes against both women and men, and says about cowboys, "They don't expect me to win, so when I do, they're very surprised. I beat nine cowboys once."

Today, rodeo remains a popular spectator sport, with about twenty-three million people attending some seven hundred rodeos annually. An additional forty million people watch the sport on television. Some of the participants are women. The WPRA (Women's Professional Rodeo Association) has more than two thousand members, with all-women's events such as bareback and bull riding, calf roping, and team roping. There are eight hundred all-women rodeos annually, with prize money totaling

Cowgirl Hall of Famer Jan Youren, age sixty, still rides bareback in rodeos. CENTER: Sandra Russell rides bareback in chaps such as these. RIGHT: Jan Youren's granddaughter Tavia Stevenson is following the family tradition of riding bulls and bareback.

"I'm in the Money"

BY CHRISTINE EWERT

~ ✶ ~

"I'm in the money; rodeo's in me.
I just won a big show, honey, can't you see.
Hello, brand new saddle,
Goodbye, rusty truck.
Now I can pay buddy; I still owe him a buck."

Tasha Stevenson gets ready to ride bareback at a rodeo in White River, South Dakota.

four million dollars. By 1993, WPRA member and barrel racing champ Charmayne James Rodman had won more than one million dollars in more than a decade of competing in rodeos.

Some women spend their lives working with horses in other ways. They break and train them, teach horseback riding, and work as veterinarians. Others compete in horse shows in activities that real "cowponies" do on the ranch, such as separating calves from the herd, a technique known as "cutting." Families can vacation at guest (or dude) ranches, where cowgirls work and lead trail rides.

Museums such as the Autry National Center of the American West in Los Angeles, and the National Cowboy Museum and Hall of Fame in Oklahoma City, include exhibits on important women of the West.

In 1975, the Cowgirl Hall of Fame was established in tiny Hereford, Texas. Its stated mission was to "honor and document the lives of women who have distinguished themselves while exemplifying the pioneer spirit of the American West." In June 2002, the expanded National Cowgirl Museum and Hall of Fame opened its doors in Fort Worth, Texas. There,

Scottie McTeer, about to leave the "chute" on a bucking horse.

"I always had horses, but my parents didn't want me to rodeo because they thought the world of rodeo wasn't the best place for a young lady. [After I got married] my father in law gave me an outstanding young horse. I trained him to run barrels. I started rodeoing. I love horses. And I guess I'm a competitor. And if you're female and want to compete on horseback, barrel racing is the way to go. So that's the way I went."

~ Carol Goosetree, horse trainer and
world champion barrel racer

The National Cowgirl Museum and Hall of Fame honors women of the West.

the newly constructed, handsome museum boasts a research library, a rare photography collection, and extraordinary exhibits, including outfits worn by Gail Davis when she played Annie Oakley, the real Annie Oakley's gun, Dale Evans's silver saddle, and tack used by famous rodeo cowgirls. Several galleries honor women in rodeo, ranching, entertainment, and western settlement. In addition, educational exhibits explain the types of work cowgirls do. Every fall, a new group of women is inducted into the Cowgirl Hall of Fame.

The Fort Worth museum's founding president, philanthropist Kit T. Moncrief, says, "We're cowgirls too. They put me on a horse when I was a baby. At first, I cried. Then they tried to take me off. I cried much louder." The museum took as its motto the philosophy of Connie Douglas Reeves: "Always saddle your own horse." At age one hundred, she was among the

Connie Douglas Reeves at the opening day parade for the National Cowgirl Museum and Hall of Fame, June 2002.

participants of a festive rodeo-style parade that celebrated the museum's opening. Connie loved horses all her life. She had learned to ride before she could walk. Beginning in the 1930s, she operated her own horse stable in San Antonio, Texas, and began giving riding lessons at Camp Waldemar for Girls. At age eighty, she retired as head riding instructor

2003 Cowgirl Hall of Fame honorees (from left to right)
Glenna Goodacre, Sheila Varian, Ann Seacrest Hanson, and
Garlene Parris, the daughter of honoree Velda Tindall Smith.

after teaching some thirty thousand campers how to handle a horse. But she continued to enjoy life on horseback for another twenty-three years. In 2002, at the Cowgirl Museum opening, she talked about how much she loved "the wide open spaces and free fresh air of the West, where one can take an early morning gallop across dew-drenched fields, and lie down to sleep beneath the star-twinkling sky, only to be awakened by the crowing of a lone rooster in the far distance."

Every year, the National Cowgirl Museum and Hall of Fame sponsors educational events, including Cowgirl 101 camp for girls and Cowgirl University for adults. Both teach roping, riding skills, and other aspects of cowgirl life over a weekend. Cowgirl Hall of Famers are the instructors. One reporter who attended later wrote, "Before Cowgirl U, I had thought of cowgirls as a kitschy symbol of Americana. But after two days in their company, I want to be one."

Being a cowgirl, after all, never goes out of style.

Bibliography

Brown, Dee. *The Gentle Tamers: Women of the Old Wild West.* Lincoln: University of Nebraska Press, 1981.

Burbick, Joan. *Rodeo Queens: On the Circuit with America's Cowgirls.* New York: Public Affairs, 2002.

Cleaveland, Agnes Morley. *No Life for a Lady.* Lincoln: University of Nebraska Press, 1977.

Crandall, Judy. *Cowgirls: Early Images and Collectibles.* Atglen, Pa.: Schiffer Publishing, 1994.

Drago, Gail. *Etta Place: Her Life and Times with Butch Cassidy and the Sundance Kid.* Plano: Republic of Texas Press, 1996.

Flood, Elizabeth Clair. *Cowgirls: Women of the Wild West.* Santa Fe, N.M.: Zion International Publishing, 2000.

George-Warren, Holly. *Cowboy: How Hollywood Invented the Wild West.* Pleasantville, N.Y.: Reader's Digest, 2002.

———. *Public Cowboy No. 1: The Life and Times of Gene Autry.* New York: Oxford University Press, 2007.

George-Warren, Holly, and Michelle Freedman. *How the West Was Worn.* New York: Harry N. Abrams, 2001.

Gilchriest, Gail. *The Cowgirl Companion: Big Skies, Buckaroos, Honky Tonks, Lonesome Blues, and Other Glories of the True West.* New York: Hyperion, 1993.

Green, Douglas B. *Singing in the Saddle: The History of the Singing Cowboy.* Nashville: Vanderbilt University Press/Country Music Foundation Press, 2003.

Havighurst, Walter. *Annie Oakley of the Wild West.* Edison, N.J.: Castle Books, 2003.

Jordan, Teresa. *Cowgirls: Women of the American West,* revised edition. Lincoln: University of Nebraska Press, 1992.

Kasson, Joy S. *Buffalo Bill's Wild West: Celebrity, Memory, and Popular History.* New York: Hill and Wang, 2000.

Kazanjian, Howard, and Chris Enss. *The Cowboy and the Senorita: A Biography of Roy Rogers and Dale Evans.* Guilford, Conn.: Twodot/Globe Pequot Press, 2004.

Kennedy, Billy. *Women of the Frontier.* Greenville, S.C.: Ambassador Publications, 2004.

Luchetti, Cathy, and Carol Olwell. *Women of the West.* New York: Orion Books/Crown, 1982.

McLeRoy, Sherrie S. *Red River Women.* Plano: Republic of Texas Press, 1996.

Montana, Patsy, with Jane Frost. *Patsy Montana: The Cowboy's Sweetheart.* Jefferson, N.C.: McFarland & Co., 2002.

Moyer, Donn J. *Cowpokes 'n' Cowbelles of the Movies and Early TV.* Tacoma, Wash.: WildWest Publishing, 2003.

O'Brien, Mary Barmeyer. *Heart of the Trail: The Stories of Eight Wagon Train Women.* Helena, Mont.: Twodot, 1997.

Peavey, Linday, and Ursula Smith. *Frontier Women.* New York: Barnes & Noble, 1996.

Riley, Glenda, and Richard W. Etulain. *By Grit and Grace: Eleven Women Who Shaped the American West.* Golden, Colo.: Fulcrum, 1997.

Roach, Joyce Gibson. *The Cowgirls.* University of North Texas Press, 1990.

Rogers, Dale Evans. *Dale: My Personal Picture Album.* Old Tappan, N.J.: Fleming H. Revell, 1971.

Rogers, Roy, and Dale Evans, with Jane and Michael Stern. *Happy Trails: Our Life Story.* New York: Simon and Schuster, 1994.

Rogers, Roy, Jr., with Karen Ann Wojahn. *Growing Up with Roy and Dale.* Ventura, Calif.: Regal Books, 1986.

Rogers-Barnett, Cheryl, and Frank Thompson. *Cowboy Princess.* Lanham, Md.: Taylor, 2003.

Rutter, Michael. *Wild Bunch Women.* Guilford, Conn.: Twodot/Globe Pequot, 2003.

Ryan, Jim. *The Rodeo and Hollywood: Rodeo Cowboys and Western Actors in the Arena.* Jefferson, N.C.: McFarland & Company, 2006.

Savage, Candace. *Cowgirls.* Berkeley, Calif.: Ten Speed Press, 1996.

Seagraves, Anne. *Daughters of the West.* Hayden, Ind.: Wesanne Publications, 1996.

Sorensen, Lorin. *Old Time Rodeo: The Way It Was.* Santa Rosa, Calif.: Silverado Publishing Co., 2008.

Stratton, Joanna L. *Pioneer Women: Voices from the Kansas Frontier.* New York: Simon & Schuster, 1981.

Tinkley, Lon, and Allen Maxell, editors. *The Cowboy Reader.* New York: David Mckay, 1959.

Wallis, Michael. *The Real Wild West: The 101 Ranch and the Creation of the American West.* New York: St. Martin's Griffin, 1999.

Western Writers Association, editors. *The Women Who Made the West.* Garden City, N.Y.: Doubleday, 1980.

Wills, Kathy Lynn, and Virginia Artho. *Cowgirl Legends from the Cowgirl Hall of Fame.* Salt Lake City: Gibbs-Smith, 1995.

Wood-Clark, Sarah. *Beautiful Daring Western Girls: Women of the Wild West.* Billings, Mont.: Buffalo Bill Historical Center, 1991. An exhibition catalogue.

Photography Sources
and Credits

Arizona Historical Society: 23

Autry National Center of the American West: vi, 73

Autry Qualified Trust/Gene Autry Entertainment: 66 (top left, middle); 70 (top), 71 (top), 72, 75, 76

Buffalo Bill Museum and Grave, Golden, Colorado: xi, 11, 27, 28, 29, 30, 31, 33, 36, 90

Buffalo Bill Ranch State Historical Park, North Platte, Nebraska: 32, 52

Courtesy of Devon Dawson: 78

John Buttram/Zella Fuller collection: 66 (bottom left)

Eleanor and Richard Eaton collection: 48, 49, 54, 84, 85 (top), 89 (center left, bottom left)

Holly George-Warren collection: v, 8, 12, 14, 18, 21, 34, 35, 42, 53, 62, 65, 66 (top right, bottom right), 68, 69, 70 (bottom), 71 (bottom), 78 (top), 81, 85 (bottom), 86, 87, 89 (center left, bottom left, bottom right)

Margie Greve: 17, 61, 108, 109

Rhonda Hole: 102 (bottom), 103

Huntington Library collection: 6

Jean Laughton (www.jeanlaughton.com): 93, 94, 95, 97, 98, 99, 100

Library of Congress: 19 (top), 25

Courtesy of Janet McBride: 79

National Cowgirl Museum and Hall of Fame, Fort Worth, Texas: 3, 7, 22, 38, 39, 43, 44, 45, 46, 47, 50, 51, 52, 55, 56, 59, 63, 82, 83, 89 (top right), 102 (top)

Deb Parker collection: 89 (center right)

Bruce Peterson collection: 19 (bottom), 20, 64

Carol Zaloom: 5, 41, 104–5, 106

Acknowledgments

Thanks so much to the many individuals who helped bring this book to life: my editor at Houghton Mifflin, Margaret Raymo, and her colleagues Erica Zappy and Sheila Smallwood; designer extraordinaire Ellen Nygaard; artists Margie Greve, Carol Zaloom, and Bob Wade; photographer Jean Laughton; museum curators Tricia Dixon (of the National Cowgirl Museum and Hall of Fame) and Steve Friesen (of the Buffalo Bill Museum and Grave); Marva Felchlin and Marilyn Kim at the Autry National Center of the American West; Karla Buhlman, Maxine Hansen, and Irynne Isip at Gene Autry

Entertainment; Steve Kemper of the Buffalo Bill Ranch State Historical Park; collectors Deb Parker, Richard and Eleanor Eaton, and Bruce Peterson; and others whose generosity and aid I greatly appreciate: the Saddle Vamps Ann Buttram and Zella Fuller; John Buttram; Susan Carlson; Barb Redfield; Lisa Wade; Deb O'Nair; Amy Hoban; Katy K and Curtis Hawkins; Bob Oermann and Mary Bufwack; Brenda Colladay; Emmy Lou Prescott; Devon Dawson; Janet McBride; Ranger Doug Green; Cheryl Rogers-Barnett; Dusty Rogers; Mary Bassel; Trine Mitchum; Sarah Lazin; and Damien Toman. As always, I couldn't have written this book without the love and support of Robert and Jack Warren. And thanks a million to those heroic cowgirls who have inspired me greatly.

~ Holly George-Warren
October 2009

Index

Page numbers in *italic* type refer to photographs or their captions.

Rodeo Ben, 83, 85
rodeos
    barrel racing, 58, 101
    bronc riding, 44, 44, 46–48,
        55, 56–58, 59, 95
    bulldogging (steer roping),
        44, 53–54, 63
    chariot racing, 48–50
    early contestants, 33, 41–43,
        42, 46, 47
    fatal accident, 56
    origin of, 41
    popularity of, 98
    prizes, 41, 44, 46, 98–100
    program cover for, 48
    stunts and trick riding,
        45–46, 48–53, 56, 56
    women, exclusion of, 41, 43,
        56–58
    women, inclusion of, 2,
        41–45, 49, 53, 54, 100
    women-only contests, 58,
        98–99
Rodman, Charmayne James,
    100
Rogers, Roy, 66–70, 68
Rogers, Will, 36
Roosevelt, Teddy, 36
Runyon, Damon, 81
Russel, Sandra, 99
rustlers, 10, 24–25
Ryan, Sheila, 66, 67

S
saddles and riding styles, 6, 10
Sawyer, Fern, 57
scouts, 6, 18, 20
Serpa, Louise, 97–98
Seymour, Jane, 65
Shaffer, Annie, 41
show girls. See Wild West
    shows
sidesaddle riding, 6
singers
    composers, 70, 77
    in movies, 65, 65–71, 67, 78
    on radio, 75, 75

    touring and recording
        performers, 72, 72–77,
        73, 76
    yodelers, 72, 72, 77–79, 78, 79
Singing Hill, The, 67
Sitting Bull, 29
Skull, Sally, 9
Smith, Lillian F. (Wenona), 34
Smith, Velda Tindall, 103
Sorrell, Lisa, 90
stagecoach driver, 9
Stanwyck, Barbara, 64, 64–65
Starr, Belle, 17–19, 19, 61
Starr, Sam, 17–18
Steele, Fanny Sperry, 45, 46,
    46, 47
steer roping (bulldogging), 44,
    53–54, 63
Stephenson, Bess, 91
Stevenson, Tavia, 99, 100
Stewart, Elinore Pruitt, 16
Stewart, Peggy, 66
Storey, June, 66
Strickland, Mabel, 38, 42, 45,
    60, 62, 63
stunts and trick riding
    in movies, 61–62, 63, 65
    in rodeos, 45–46, 48–53, 56,
        56
    in Wild West shows, 29, 32,
        34–35, 37, 38
Sundance Kid, 24

T
television shows, 65, 67, 71–72
Texas Rose, 33
Texas Trailhands, 78
trick riding. See stunts and
    trick riding

U
Union Pacific, 64

V
Varian, Sheila, 103

W
Walker, Cindy, 67
Watson, Ellen, 10
Wenona (Lillian F. Smith), 34
Westerns. See movies and
    television shows
westward migration. See
    pioneer women
Wild Bunch, 23–24
Wild West shows
    acts and stunts, 29, 32, 34–35,
        37, 38
    Buffalo Bill's Wild West
        Show, 27, 29–32, 30,
        31, 32, 34
    Congress of Rough Riders
        and Ropers, 36–38
    costumes, 35, 36
    Kemp Sisters' Wild West
        Show, 33
    Miller Brothers 101 Ranch
        Wild West Show, 33,
        33–38, 34, 35, 38, 61
    Pawnee Bill's Wild West,
        30, 32–33
    pay, 30, 31, 37
    performers, 30
    Texas Kid Wild West
        Show, 33
    women-owned shows, 33
Wilkins, Kitty, 10–12
Williams, Lizzie Johnson, 10
Williamson, Kim, 58
WLS National Barn Dance,
    75–77, 76
Women's Professional Rodeo
    Association (WPRA),
    58, 98–100
Woodend, Jennie, 34–35
Woody's Roundup Featuring
    Riders in the Sky, 78
Wyoming, women's rights in,
    12–13

yodelers, 72, 72, 77–79, 78, 79
Younger, Cole, 17
Youren, Jan, 99

 Holly George-Warren is an award-winning writer, editor, producer, and music consultant. She has contributed to more than two dozen books about rock-and-roll, including *The New Rolling Stone Encyclopedia of Rock & Roll, The Rolling Stone Book of Women in Rock,* and *The Rolling Stone Illustrated History of Rock & Roll.* She's also written for the *New York Times,* the *Village Voice,* the *Journal of Country Music,* and *Rolling Stone.* Ms. George-Warren lives in upstate New York with her family. Visit her online at **www.hollygeorgewarren.com.**